DIVINATION BY MAGIC

**Secret instructions of an Esoteric Lodge, contained in
letters from an initiate to a neophyte, on the secrets of
pendulum magic and the ancient art of scrying.**

DIVINATION
BY
MAGIC

**Taken by Noud van den Eerenbeemt from the
instructions of an Esoteric Lodge**

Introduction by W.N. Schors

Translated from the Dutch by Transcript, Ltd.

SAMUEL WEISER, INC.
York Beach, Maine

First published in Holland by
Uitgeverij Schors, Amsterdam
Original title: *Pendel-, Kristal- En Speigelmagie*

First published in English in 1982 by
The Aquarian Press, Wellingborough, England
under the title: *The Pendulum, Crystal Ball and Magic Mirror*

First American edition 1985 by
Samuel Weiser, Inc.
Box 612
York Beach, Maine 03910

ISBN 0-87728-597-7
Library of Congress Catalog Card Number: 85-50790
Translated by Transcript, Ltd., Clevedon, England

Printed in the United States of America by
McNaughton & Gunn, Inc.
Ann Arbor, MI

CONTENTS

INTRODUCTION

The pendulum, crystal ball and metal mirror are outstanding magical aids because they serve to make known to an individual facts and phenomena which are hidden from him and so enable him to increase his knowledge or power as the case may be. Nevertheless, between the pendulum on one hand and the crystal ball and magic mirror on the other there is considerable difference in origin and purpose. The pendulum is derived from the divining rod, a magical instrument in the form of a forked twig, which in the hands of those who are able to use it can indicate the presence of minerals or water under the earth's surface by making spasmodic movements of varying intensity. From antiquity (Cicero and Tacitus for example) right down to relatively modern times (Agricola, Robert Boyle, Locke, etc.) no doubts were entertained concerning the trustworthiness of the method. An especially important part was played by the divining rod in mining operations carried out in the Hartz Mountains and in Sudetenland. What is more, this type of dowsing was a decisive factor in locating springs and in sinking wells. According to the most celebrated authority in this field, the priest and natural philosopher P. de Vallemont (1649-1721), the divining rod forms a natural compensation for the instinct now lost to man (though not to the animals) for finding life-sustaining water at all times. More recently we encounter the divining rod in speleological investigations. Thus in 1920 for example the famous cave complex at Eyzies-de-Tayac in the Dordogne, known as 'Le Grand Roc', was discovered on indications given by the expert A. Viré.

Since the divining rod by virtue of its shape and size, its degree of sensitivity and mode of operation, is more suitable for work in the open air, the need arose for a magical instrument that would exhibit the properties of the divining rod to best advantage in a closed room. Thus the pendulum was developed. A pendulum normally consists of a long thin thread supporting a heavy bob, the shape of which may vary from sphere, cylinder, plummet and disc to spiral. Ever since Paracelsus at the beginning of the sixteenth century introduced the word 'sidereal' into magic to designate facts and phenomena originating in forces beyond the range of observation, the pendulum has frequently been called the 'sidereal pendulum'. The 'body' of the pendulum is usually made of metal, and preferably of an alloy of the seven planetary metals, so as to interpose a measure of neutrality between the dowser and the object of his search. In contrast to the fairly sluggish and unwieldy rod, which takes time to act, the pendulum is a very quick, extremely mobile instrument that registers mainly 'foreign' or interfering influences, to which it is as sensitive as the anemometer is to wind. Hence the divining rod is more adapted to finding those reservoirs of force which have been in existence for a long time (water springs, minerals) whereas the chief use of the pendulum is in identifying new, intrusive elements (diseases). Generally speaking, *the divining rod has a creative, the pendulum a corrective function.*

As far as the reliability of the pendulum is concerned, the facts speak for themselves: from time immemorial pendulists have been consulted with considerable success by industrial firms and by medical and even military authorities. In France the 'radiesthesist' is recognized as an expert in his field and his advice is taken into consideration with that of other specialists, not sought as a last resort.

It is regrettable that not enough has been made of the Tarot as an aid to dowsing. Because at each moment the Tarot can show us a faithful representation of our personalities and can indicate to us those states of consciousness which govern our personalities, it is therefore able to impart an extra element of precision to dowsing work.

The test person places his left hand on the table. The twenty-two Tarot trumps are then laid down a few centimetres from his hand one by one. The relationship of the test person to each card can be discovered by holding the pendulum at a height of a few centimetres between the hand and the Tarot card. There are now three possibilities. The first is that the pendulum swings backwards and forwards at right angles to an imaginary line joining the hand and the card and thus clearly separates them. In this case the card concerned is put away without further ado. At that particular time there is obviously no connection between the personality of the test person and the state of consciousness expressed by the Tarot card. The second possibility is that the pendulum swings along the imaginary line joining the hand and the card and so clearly links the two. In this case the card is set aside separately. Finally, it is possible that the pendulum will describe a circle around the hand and card. Their unity is indicated here; the card concerned reveals the state of consciousness playing the most essential role in the individual at the given moment. This card is also placed to one side.

After the same process has been repeated with all twenty-two trumps, the total of the numbers is found and this is reduced to the basic numerological number, and so the Tarot card is discovered that represents the quintessence of the personality of the test person or of the nature of the situation at the time in question. If this method, like any other, is to prove successful, the pendulist must try to be as objective as possible, i.e. he must dismiss all feelings of prejudice or preference. If this is not done, the pendulum will not swing freely in the ambivalent situation in which it has to move and so a true result will not be obtained.

Magic Mirrors and Crystal Balls

There is a difference in origin and purpose between the pendulum on one side and the crystal ball and metal mirror on the other. The use of the crystal ball and of the magic mirror (which came in vogue later) arose not through the wish to find something hidden but through the discovery that staring for some time at a shiny surface would induce a loss of conscious and of voluntary activity. This condition, known as trance, is often accompanied by clairvoyance in time and space; a state experienced as pleasant. Although this condition was originally ascribed to magical properties in the shiny article itself – since stones, metals, pools, rivers were sacred to gods or demons – the conviction slowly grew that it was the individual himself or herself who induced the condition simply by concentrating on the object, and that therefore the phenomenon could invariably be made to occur with practice.

In fact this was the start of the recognition of the value of hypnosis and of the attendant somnambulism. After somewhat tentative approaches to the subject by Aristotle, Pliny, Avicenna and Albertus Magnus, it was the brilliant Jesuit, Athanasius Kircher (1601-1680) who first gave a matter-of-fact description of the the complex phenomena of concentration, rigidity, abstraction and hallucination, in his *Ars Magnetica*. The equally brilliant Paracelsus (1493-1541) had been just as practical a century earlier in criticizing all the ceremonial mumbo jumbo that had slowly attached itself to crystal gazing. Paracelsus emphasized, and in this he was followed by J. van Helmont (1577-1644), a Belgian alchemist, that clairvoyance arose through man's inherent magnetic powers, the *magnes microcosmi*, and not through any preparatory magical ritual. Even so, to this very day crystallomancy is often preceded by magical rituals involving the usual 'props' such as swords, candles, incense, etc., while, naturally, the right astrological time for scrying is also determined.

It seems highly likely that the use of crystal balls did not enter into the first auto-hypnotic experiences of mankind. Before this there was a period in which the trance state was reached via concentrating on precious stones (especially on beryl), rings, metal beakers and in particular on transparent vessels (bowls) containing water. Genuine crystal gazing came into being in the Renaissance, when by means of concentrating on oval balls, preferably made of pure crystal, *but in any case of completely transparent glass*, hypnotic states and visionary hallucinations were produced. The inexplicable fact that the events seen during these hallucinations seemed either to have taken place elsewhere, or else were going to occur on the spot or elsewhere, was generally disputed by the medical profession. Exceptions were doctors like Mesmer (1734-1815), J. Braid (1795-1860), the father of hypnosis, and Professor Charcot (1825-1893), the teacher of Breuer and forerunner of Freud, who not only established the correctness of previous findings but used hypnosis as the basis or essential part of their theories concerning the reasons for human behaviour and the way to correct it.

The magic mirror has the same origin and object as the crystal ball, namely clairvoyance via auto-hypnosis by gazing at a shiny surface. The circumstances surrounding its employment are also very similar: from beginning to end, practices involving the magic mirror have been surrounded by rituals designed to make the scryer more intent and therefore more receptive.

These mirrors, made of metal or graphite are substitutes for the old gems, rings and crystal balls. They have an average diameter of three inches. From the numerous, extremely precise specifications for their manufacture it appears that, until the Middle Ages, the mirror was considered to be more important than the scryer. Just as in the case of precious stones, etc., the trance was ascribed to the action of the mirror and not to the soul of its user. It was not until the time of Nostradamus (1503-1566), the court magician of Catherine de' Medici, that people began to understand (under the influence of Paracelsus once again) that the process of clairvoyance depended on the psyche of the clairvoyant.

Until not so long ago this situation remained very static. The more primitive the nature of the scryer, the more dependent he felt on the ball or mirror, and the more he strove to make these magical instruments favourable to him via ritual and/or offerings. Under this type of practitioner came the raisers of spirits, i.e. those who did not believe they were personally clairvoyant but thought they were receiving communications concerning yesterday, today and tomorrow from spirit beings. Fortunately this type of person is increasingly rare in modern occultism.* Most esoteric schools emphasize to their students that it is the individual who 'sees' and that therefore it is extremely important for him to be properly instructed, well prepared and well equipped for his task before attempting crystal and mirror magic, without relying on such minor matters as ceremonies and spirits. Naturally, the same applies to the use of the pendulum, but there is less danger of the senses being deluded in this case.

Much that is inconceivable and concealed will be revealed to those who employ these three magical instruments, skilfully, deliberately and purposefully. Because this knowledge can contribute to making us more detached and tranquil in the face of the crazy and dreary spectacle we call society, pendulum, crystal and mirror magic still have a meaning for us.

---

*As will be seen from these remarks, the writer of the Introduction probably belongs to a school of thought that seeks a *rapprochement* between occultism and science. However, we should proceed very warily along this road, otherwise we might find ourselves in the grip of internal malevolent forces while disarming ourselves with the notion that all forces involved belonged to our own psyches.   *Tr.*

PART ONE: PENDULUM MAGIC
1. The Historical and Scientific Background

Dear Friend,

The results of pure scientific research into the practical and theoretical aspects of the forces behind the pendulum have tended to confirm facts long known to initiates. However, the road to a knowledge of spiritual cosmic laws is long, partly because it is followed by means of certain instruments acting as 'extension pieces' to our incompletely developed sense organs.

A totally new era is being born out of the chaos of the expiring Piscean period. Drastic changes in the planetary radiations influencing mankind are bringing forth a spiritual revolution that is making us conscious of the cosmic laws that govern the universe. Once again we are approaching zero point on the material plane; but ruin must be followed by rise! As above, so below! Your own body, itself a complete expression of the cosmos, is a symbol of knowledge and truth in every cell. The dawn of a new age is here. Under the rays of Aquarius, Uranus is already at work in those who can hear and see.

From a purely scientific point of view – that is to say, in the light of objective research from which all emotional attitudes are deliberately excluded – the sidereal pendulum is a scientific instrument that can register and measure extremely fine, invisible radiations. The path of spiritual evolution is threefold and leads through the realms of science, philosophy and mysticism. It is only by paying attention to all three of these realms that one becomes aware of the fact that together they form an indissoluble whole and that any opposition between them is apparent only.

The field of pendulum research is so wide and so closely connected with many other fields of knowledge that it is impossible to give general directives. Each investigator will elicit certain dowsing reactions according to his nature and abilities. My own experience has brought me a great deal of information concerning the pendulum detection of thoughts, thought forms, astral vibrations (due to demons and elementals) and the like. All these aspects receive scant treatment in scientific literature on the pendulum.

In spite of the most objective forms of testing, the explanations offered by the different researchers into the behaviour of the pendulum diverge from one another and at times are contradictory; nevertheless, if we take into account the individuality of each researcher, their results are generally similar.

A working hypothesis has been found for the sidereal pendulum which means that we have fixed ground rules on which each researcher who is working scientifically and objectively can build. The extensiveness and the varied nature of the terrain can, with personal intuitive insights, enlarge awareness and improve the balance between feeling and understanding.

The history of the subject reveals that the use of the pendulum goes back to antiquity. Here too materialism has tried to make a clean sweep of the old authorities, but it is only the basis of our procedures that has changed. The philosopher Schopenhauer, who showed so much feeling for mysticism, was quite right when he said, 'Before it is accepted, each problem runs through three stages. In the first stage it seems ridiculous, in the second it is opposed and in the third stage it is self-evident.'

His words are an apt description of pendulum research. At present we are still in the second stage – that of opposition. The very name sidereal pendulum raises difficulties whenever we attempt to explain its origin. The pendulum is closely connected with the dowser's ring and with the question of dowsing in general. Various names in accordance with their uses have been given to the instruments which can register radiations. Thus we have the 'sidereal pendulum', the 'geomantic ring', the 'geomantic ball', the 'rod ring', 'Goethe's pendulum', 'the water seeker' (a particularly sensitive divining rod) and so on.

Reichenbach found in all these expressions a very important source of scientific material with considerable potential. But Reichenbach confined his attention to the radiations emanated by the human body and by objects and did not know that a photograph will absorb these radiations, which can then be clearly detected by means of a pendulum. This fact was discovered much later by Kallenberg (in 1913). The name 'sidereal pendulum' appears to have been bestowed no longer ago than the middle of the last century and, in the course of time, the instrument has undergone all sorts of changes and has been made the subject of a variety of explanations. Further details on this point will be found in the works of Professor

Leopold Oelenheinz (*Der Wünschelring*, Leipzig 1920), who has made a special study of origins.

When, while conducting numerous scientific experiments with the pendulum and divining rod, people came to realize their essentially different character and how dissimilar they are in a number of respects, they began to speak of the 'pendulum' and 'sidereal pendulum'. Then, when the pendulum was later employed to study radiations from the human body, there was talk of the 'psychic pendulum'.

It is plain from a number of his works, that Goethe (whom we may consider to have been an initiate in the occult sense of the word) knew the use of the pendulum. One has only to read the second chapter in part two of *Wahlverwandschaften* (Affinities) to appreciate this. An accurate account is given there of an experiment with a pendulum which reveals his knowledge of the matter. It is worth re-reading Goethe's *Faust* in this light in order to penetrate the real meanings of the symbols employed by Goethe. The book will then become an inexhaustible source of esoteric knowledge and an aid to spiritual development. It is clear that the divining rod and pendulum were well-known articles. Perhaps Moses' staff can be explained along similar lines too, although whether it was used as a rod or swung like a pendulum is uncertain.

Pendulums were used as oracles by the civilized peoples of the Ancient World, and the Roman author Ammianus Marcellinus paints a lively picture of how the pendulum oracle was consulted during the reign of the Emperor Valentianis.

The attention of modern investigators is being drawn once more to the sidereal pendulum and the whole field is now undergoing scientific examination. In this connection, many people are trying to design instruments which are analogous to the pendulum but at the same time exclude all types of foreign influence (suggestion, involuntary hand movements, ideo-motoric movements). Their aim is to use electricity as the motive force in these instruments, which would then work entirely independently of the human body. However, the results obtained have been wide of the mark and completely inadequate.

There was also a small number of researchers who looked on the human body as the chief source of radiation and considered that physical contact with the pendulum is indispensable. And when Baron von Levetzov in his *Der siderische Pendel als Anzeiger menschlicher Charaktereigenschaften*, i.e. The Sidereal Pendulum as an Indicator of Human Character (Leipzig, 1922), treats the human body as a 'radiation pressure machine' and refers to Lord Lytton's 'Vril', he is regarding this energy as the precursor of a power now lost to us (which was once available to the inhabitants of Atlantis) and evinces profound occult and esoteric insight.

In addition to the much maligned Reichenbach, there is Professor Johann Karl von Bähr with his book *Der Dynamische Kreis*, i.e. The Dynamic Circle (1861). This work is the result of intense research and the author investigated about two thousand different substances with the help of the pendulum.

Other research workers are: Dr H. Geffcken (Fresh discoveries in the field of N-rays, starting with the discoveries of Professor Bähr and the experiments performed by Blondot in Nancy); the engineer Johannes Zacharias: *Rätsel der Natur, Verborgene Gewalten im Weltgeschehen* (The Riddle of Nature, Hidden Forces in World Affairs); Fr. Kallenberg; *Die Offenbarungen des siderischen Pendels* (The Revelations of the Sidereal Pendulum); Dr Naum Kotik, F. Feerhow: *N-rays und Od* (N-rays and Od); Dr H. Langbein: *Ergebnisse von Untersuchungen mit dem siderischen Pendel* (Results of Investigations using the Sidereal Pendulum); Dr H. Voll: *Die Wünschelrute und das siderische Pendel* (The Divining Rod and the Sidereal Pendulum); Dr Ferd. Maack: *Manuradioskop*, and many others.

The experts named here are by no means all who have engaged in pendulum research, but they are distinguished by having developed original theories of radiation and by an unprejudiced scientific zeal to go further than can be reached by the five senses, i.e. to find the connection between the material and the transcendental and to build a bridge between the two. This is a way that can be taken only *via* considerable intuitive insights however.

Having grasped some idea of the history of the pendulum it is necessary to know something about the various forms of radiation affecting the pendulum. Firstly, however, it is important to see how science explains the movement of the pendulum. Afterwards, we shall consider the laws, effects and techniques involved in pendulum work.

Those radiations with which we have to do in working with the pendulum are so subtle that the human body, which serves both as a source of radiations and as an antenna for picking them up, can behave disruptively due to bad technique, incomplete training and faulty connections, and so can vitiate your results. Perhaps this is why science looks somewhat askance at our subject, since it prefers experimenting with apparatus which is to a certain extent independent of the human body.

How then do we explain the measured movements the pendulum makes as soon as it is connected with the human body or to an electric current?

Perhaps it will be useful to briefly recall the laws governing the sidereal pendulum. In general, the pendulum is a weight made of some material or other, suspended by a thread. The foremost property of such a device is that it is always being pulled into a position of rest by the force of gravity. Only some external stimulus or a constant supply of energy – as in a pendulum clock or a magnetic pendulum – can make it oscillate. If the supply of energy ceases, the pendulum will come to rest after a while. The air produces friction and has a braking effect.

A distinction is made between the scientific and the mathematical pendulum. Both are subject to the same laws of oscillation as formulated and calculated by Galileo. The fundamental formula states that: 'The time of oscillation of a pendulum (irrespective of its length) is the square root of the inverse ratio of the intensity of the gravitational force'; 'The period of oscillation (time of oscillation) of a pendulum consists of one complete swing backwards and forwards from the starting point.'

The formula for calculating a full period is:

$$T = 2\pi\sqrt{\frac{L}{G}}$$

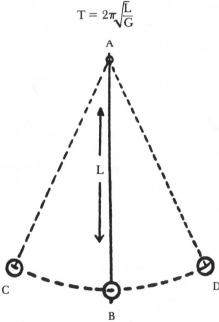

Figure 1. A – B = both the pendulum in its resting position and the length of the pendulum (as do A – C, A – D).

B – C, B – D, or C – D, D – C, as the case may be = to and fro movement.

T is the time in seconds for a complete oscillation forwards and backwards. L is the length of the pendulum in metres. G is the known acceleration due to gravity of a falling weight. It has to be calculated for each particular spot on the earth's surface. With this formula the length and period of any pendulum can be found.

The seconds pendulum is based on a manipulation of this formula to give:

$$L = \frac{G}{\pi^2} \quad \text{(when} \quad \pi\sqrt{\frac{L}{G}} = 1\text{)}$$

Therefore the pendulum is one means of determining the gravitational pull of the earth.

Although the substance of which the pendulum is made is bound to have some influence on the period of oscillation, we find that gravity acts on all materials with the same strength. This has been confirmed by experiments performed in a vacuum. The seconds pendulum has further shown that the earth is flattened at the poles. This was pointed out by Richter as long ago as 1672. He noticed variations in the period from place to place and drew the correct conclusion, that the gravitational pull of the earth must decrease from the equator to the poles. The formula he discovered is hardly important for our purposes. Figure 1 will help you to understand the formula for the scientific pendulum that was given earlier. A–B is the pendulum at rest and also the length of the pendulum. The same applies to A–C and A–D. B–C, B–D and D–C show the swing.

It is a generally known fact that certain natural laws and cosmic phenomena were originally misunderstood or not understood at all and so were regarded as supernatural. Slowly they evolved in the human mind, originally in the fantasy of several leading spirits, who were mocked and persecuted by the scientists of the day. Then, as facts accumulated, they were taken up by the man in the street, and eventually were recognized and accepted as good and reasonable hypotheses.

All great discoveries and rediscoveries were once regarded as idle imagination and humbug and were relegated to the land of fables. Examples of what we are talking about can be found in belief in spirits, electrical technology, magnetism and pendulum dowsing. Astrology is a precisely similar case. Man is a child of his times even where spiritual insight is concerned. The things that in antiquity were thought of as forces and powers deployed by the heathen gods were seen in the Middle Ages as properties belonging to God and the Devil. Our own age seeks to explain all the problems of life with such concepts as body and mind, force and matter. Not so long ago these ideas were influenced by theories of radiation and emanation which came to the fore during research into radium; the results pain-stakingly accumulated by Reichenbach on the subject of Od seemed to be confirmed by scientific investigation.

These radiations, which occur everywhere in the universe and fill the entire cosmos, are what Indians term the world ether. They range from the rays of the largest sun, named Algol by astronomers and which is three hundred times bigger than our own Sun, to the force-field around the atom of radium. Since they are apparent to our sense organs they form part of material reality.

We can explain the phenomenon of the sidereal pendulum in terms of this primeval force-field, considered as the Principle of all things. Physics and chemistry are two important pillars of science, but they are concerned mainly with radiations from inorganic matter (magnetism, electricity, heat, light, actinic rays producing chemical changes, etc.). The virtue of Reichenbach's experiments was to demonstrate radiations coming from organic matter and to reveal the possibility of a radiation physics covering that area too.

The X-rays of Röntgen, the alpha, beta and gamma rays of radium, delta rays, P and N rays (Blondot), ultra-violet radiation and the Y rays of Professor Yurevitch of Moscow – all these are demonstrably present even though they are invisible.

One may theorize that the cosmos arose out of a force field (the world ether), which manifests itself in various ways in the world of appearances. Its manifestations may be either constructive or destructive. Every movement, even the least, is the product of some impulse or cause. In an exoteric sense forces are substances in motion, but in an esoteric sense they are vibrations of the world ether. We learn from astrology that via the heavenly bodies (the Sun, the fixed stars and the planets) we receive light, spectroscopic information and astrological influences.

By means of nothing more than a given potential, a certain force can be brought into being. This potential naturally strives for release, neutralization and dissipation, often giving the impression of a condensed ball of energy. Tension release is governed by fixed laws, which may produce spectacular effects as in the electrical discharges during a thunderstorm or the explosion of a keg of gunpowder. The most compressed energy is immediately released on neutralization, as happens with light, heat and water power. The phenomenon of the pendulum is a case in point. Physics has now discovered that all bodies emit vibrations of various frequencies and strengths.

For example, if I were to hold a pendulum above a piece of metal, the pendulum would start to move. It would be necessary to exclude all negative influences beforehand, but more of that later. It follows that each movement presupposes the presence of a certain force and that the latter is due to a state of tension. The principle involved is that of action and reaction.

The phenomena observable with a pendulum, which to a certain extent are the same as those seen with the divining rod, indicate that the movement is brought about by kinetic propulsion and produces an output of work.

The sidereal pendulum does not swing in a fixed direction, but describes all sorts of oscillatory figures, which are dependent on the nature of the material being dowsed. Official science has no explanation to offer for this. A simple directional force such as magnetism would pull the pendulum to one side but would not keep it in continual motion.

Looking now at the nature of electricity, we can take a further step. Here we have to do with polarity, in which the poles exhibit attraction and repulsion: attraction between + and –, saturation with ++ and repulsion between like poles. Similar effects lie at the basis of the phenomena of the sidereal pendulum. Nevertheless, continuous motion of the pendulum occurs only when there is a question of changing potential and changing polarities. Not until then does amplitude come into the picture.

The impulses that create the motion cannot reside in the objects over which the pendulum is held and even less can they reside in the cosmic radiations within the great etheric force field; otherwise it would be impossible for the instrument to keep still. Only when an animal factor is added to the radiation does the pendulum swing noticeably.

The cause of this phenomenon is in the radiation of Od, such as takes place from the human body.

And here we have reached the point where opinions are divided. The following considerations will make clear in what way our bodies can function as a source of radiations for the sidereal pendulum.

That the body's magnetism cannot be the cause of the pendulum's movements has already been remarked. Nevertheless, it does have something to do with what we call the Ether, and Goethe had an inkling of this when he spoke of magnetism as a primary phenomenon.

When we look at the remarkable patterns made by the lines of force of variously shaped coils and magnets, we are impressed with the extraordinary regularity of the magnetic field.

Research has shown that the human Od-field, when strengthened by electricity and thus channelled into more chemical activities, has exactly the same kind of force field and lines of force. However, it is possible to make another inference at this point and it is this, that the neutral zone to which so little attention has so far been paid is the most essential one in magnetism and that the poles should really only be regarded as emission points. This has led Dr Ferdinand Maack to the following conclusion: 'All bodies are surrounded by invisible movements' and: 'Neutrality is the only active element'.

Everything is vibration and radiation. In, around, above and below us, before and behind us, everything is in perpetual motion. *Prana*, the Akasha principle of Indian occult lore, which is the creative, constructive and also destructive universal principle, is the same thing as that 'neutrality' of which science speaks.

This energizing force that produces vibrations in the electrons, ions and atoms of matter in accordance with natural law, strives to express itself as fully as possible. For this purpose, electricity runs through wire, magnetism spreads out from steel and bio-energy uses protoplasm.

Therefore Zacharias was right when he stated: 'Bodies possess no inherent power of movement, but continually receive it from without.'

The real principle of activity thus lies outside objects; these, including the human body, are merely transformers of which external forces make use.

That is the insight obtained by present-day science into these matters, and it is precisely what was discovered by Indian mystics, who have never accepted that magnetism resides in iron or that thoughts are manufactured by the brain or that life is a product of somatic cells. Our bodies are nothing more than transformers employed by the world ether. They are endowed with certain centres through which the *Prana* is received and distributed; the secret underlying this interaction being the transformation of one thing into another.

Returning now to the sidereal pendulum, we see that that too is simply a transformation apparatus for the human Od. Unless this fact is appreciated we shall be blinded by false mysticism and be unable to explain its movements in accordance with scientific laws. The principle at work is extremely simple: we pass current through an electric motor and receive in return rotation, power and motion. Something of the same sort occurs with the pendulum: we supply the pendulum with Od and thus provoke a mechanical movement governed by natural law. What is so hard to understand about that?

Admittedly, science is unable to tell us just what kind of force this Od really is, but can it do any better where electricity is concerned? We are surrounded on all sides by 'unknown' forces known to us only by their effects. That great initiate Goethe has this to say about it: 'The highest happiness of man is to study those things which are open to investigation and to reverence those things which are not.'

By the movement it makes, the pendulum exhibits a tendency to describe circles and ellipses, just like the paths of the planets. These paths and the formulas which they have in common with the pendulum and with gravitation, all point in the direction of the great secret of the number that (although still unsolved) plays a universal role – the number π.

The basic movement of the pendulum is in a circle. Anyone who notices the striking connection here with π^2 and with gravitational effects (acceleration) will see what a range of ideas it opens up. In particular, he will see how closely bound up the pendulum is with cosmic laws, and how these laws express themselves in its activity. Just as this mysterious number pi serves as a matrix for the spherical and circular forms, so is the secret of the formation of the world ether hidden within it, and this world ether is itself the matrix for all the shapes, forces and principles to be found on earth.

Thus the latent image of the microcosm lies in the macrocosm. As above, so below. These are profound concepts, but inferable nevertheless from the very existence of the number pi.

The old lore has once again been confirmed by modern science. The material universe is a projection of the cosmos; it is a mirror image which the cosmos forms and contains within itself. It is gratifying to learn how close occult and official science have come to one another.

We must now consider the theory of latent images in the world ether. In mental phenomena, such as consciousness, memory, emotion and the like, no adequate explanation can be found in the processes of inorganic chemistry (only materialists equate brain and intellect!). We are obliged to postulate the existence of latent images in the world ether to account for physical forces and chemical elements. These latent images do, in fact, bear some analogy with the chemical elements, although we must never lose sight of the unity of existence behind the elements. All forms, principles and powers have their being in this world ether and they become 'actual' to us through the medium of suitable 'transformers'. For example, certain principles find their expression as thoughts in the brain that is tuned in to their particular 'wavelength'. Hence the source of all life and growth does not lie in our Earth or in some substance or other but in the world ether.

The secret of life lies in the elaboration of all these interactions of varying intensity, such as arise through the operation of the Law of Polarity. On the assumption that latent images exist in the world ether, all activity on earth is merely a projection or impression of such latent images.

The leading principle in the world ether is the electron, the ion. These electrons, laden with the life-force of the ether, form the building bricks of matter and also carry the spores of that spiritual principle-of-all-forms which manifests in and outside us in physical, emotional and mental functions.

From all this we can draw the following conclusions with regard to the pendulum:

If we postulate that all natural laws and their operations have been present in the world ether from all eternity, we can view the pendulum not only as a transformer but also as an instrument that vibrates with and resonates with those forces and energies which are easily released from the astral body of man, and reacts on similar forces in specific objects (magnetism).

However, we can deepen these conclusions still further and become involved in profound occult ideas which play a part in traditions going back for thousands of years. There are powers of memory and powers that lie hidden to the soul. And as above (we have quoted this before) so below, or shall we say, as below so above? When these powers fall from the macrocosm on unprepared, ignorant people, they suffer from mental cramp and emotional disturbances, which then express themselves in the form of megalomania, passion, delusions of grandeur and genius, insanity, possession, spontaneous astral projection, etc. This is why in the occult systems of India such stress is laid on not attracting such powers lightly. Anyone who does not perceive the essential character of Saturn, the 'Dweller on the Threshold', will come to regret it. It is fatal to expose oneself to the influence of certain radiations without having activated the corresponding force centre in one's own personality. All thoughts and memories are nothing but vibrations coming from this infinite ether sea.

But there is a bridge which leads us into that realm. Think of the Indian teaching concerning thought forms. Think of the so-called Akashic records in which are stored all the vibrations that have ever been produced. Those who have developed the gifts of clairvoyance or clairaudience can 'tune in' to this reservoir of vibrations and can abstract information from it.

Everything you do with the material form and action of the pendulum can be improved by mechanical refinements, but everything else is concerned with vibrations and is supplied to it by the person in whose hand it is being held. If this person succeeds in drawing something out of the depths of the etheric sea, as many have done before him and as many are still doing today, it will be due to his own proficiency and skill. Since contact with this 'other side' of existence is quite rare in the normal waking state and usually occurs in sleep and dreams or in trances, one must be thoroughly aware of the many dangers which threaten those who dabble in mediumship and magic. Thus it is of the utmost importance – even when dealing with such an apparently harmless thing as the pendulum – that you keep on extending your knowledge of this field.

I want to return now to the thought that electrons are the intermediaries between heaven and earth. Every vibration causes some movement. Vibration is a force and each force encounters resistance in the form of friction. The world of events is simply a reaction between the two opposites, vibration and friction. In the material sector of the universe, we know that sound, light waves, vibrations, magnetic fields and electric currents are the mutual relationships between the chemical elements (attractions and repulsions), their affinities and so on. In the psychic sector, we have to do with dreams, emotions, 'atmospheres' and such phenomena as second sight. All these things proceed not from ourselves but from the etheric sea of the cosmos, the existence of which can be explained quite logically. Anyone who has acquired the necessary skills, can verify this for himself.

Reichenbach employed the pendulum in his researches to obviate human error. Not everyone is sensitive enough for or constitutionally suited to making clairvoyant observations, for example. Therefore certain instruments have been chosen as 'go-betweens', and the pendulum is one of these.

As Martin Ziefler has shown, the Od radiations play a big part in all this. In order to demonstrate the existence of these radiations without trusting to impressions, he availed himself of a remarkable piece of apparatus. He experimented on the fine hairs of the sundew, a carnivorous plant that grows in marshy places. It has no instinct by which it chooses its food but it reacts to the radiations emitted by small animals. Ziefler found that the plant bent eagerly towards a piece of platinum irradiated with Od, but did not touch an insect that had been deprived of its radiation.

Blondot and Charpentier are two research workers who also studied Od radiations. They are well known for their polarization experiments and they named the vibrations whose existence they had demonstrated, N-rays. The magnetiser Tornim succeeded in 1891 in photographing radiation from hands.

Similar tests were carried out by Professor Rapp at the Academy of Arts, Düsseldorf. Dr Harnack discovered that the skin radiates electricity and he was able to move with one finger a magnetic needle which was under glass.

I could quote many more examples of the same kind to illustrate the progress made by investigators in this field. Increasing efforts are being made to prove the existence of radiations of this sort by physical and chemical means. You will probably find it helpful if I give you some details of twentieth-century developments. The radiation from the human body has become a popular topic both in occult and in scientific literature and it has been the subject of numerous reports and discussions.

The radium content of the human body was demonstrated by research worker A. Caan of Frankfurt in a paper emanating from the University of Heidelberg in 1911. His tests showed that photographic plates were affected by these radiations and that the air is ionized by human organs (both before and after cremation), and that therefore atomic disintegration is continually going on inside us with a consequent production of radiations.

The phenomenon is comparable with the Od of Reichenbach. Since atomic fission does not occur at the same rate in each human body, the radiation from each individual's body also differs from that emitted by others. Presumably, atomic activity and radiation is particularly strong in so-called 'sensitives'. Anyway, such people are especially good with the pendulum; they possess the power to raise the necessary potential.

Another important article was published in 1926 by the *Zentralblatt für Okkultismus*, commenting on reports of a number of interesting experiments written by Professor Ferdinand Cazzamali of the University of Milan for the *Revue Metaphysique*. He established quite conclusively that the human brain sends out electromagnetic waves after the fashion of a radio transmitter. These waves emitted by the brain can be received. Professor Cazzamali gathered several test subjects in one room and got them to perform mental work, and he was able to pick up in a special apparatus the waves sent out by their brains. Thus it has been possible to register mental power by mechanical means.

Professor Cazzamali thought he had solved the problem of telepathy by means of his researches. These human 'brain waves' (if we may call them that) are of great intensity and their transmission possibilities are practically unlimited. The important point is for the nervous system of the receiver to be tuned in to the same wavelength as that of the sender. Once these results of pure scientific research have been confirmed by further investigations along the same lines, we shall see all sorts of facts known to the spiritual sciences for thousands of years upheld by natural philosophy.

For the student of the occult, it is important to control the mind and body so that one is in a position to tune in to every cosmic or human 'wavelength', otherwise it is impossible to become proficient in the use of the pendulum.

All our examples presage an eventual synthesis of natural and occult science. Here is a foundation on which we may safely build an understanding of the pendulum and everything to do with it. By setting out from the above starting point, we shall escape from the rigid dogmatism of official science on the one hand and from the cloud of fantasy and naivety that so often envelopes occultism on the other hand. Each of these is unfruitful in its own way.

In our own investigations into pendulum magic, we shall rely on those two poles of the human personality – the feelings and the emotions – to penetrate to the centre of our own nature and to that of the cosmos.

2. The Practice of Pendulum Dowsing

After this introduction to the forces that lie behind the pendulum, we can now start looking at some practical details. It should be clear to you that the regime you have been following has been necessary to make you sufficiently sensitive to use the pendulum. However, there are certain astrological indications which will tell you whether you have an aptitude for using the instrument. As with other occult (or indeed artistic) occupations, it is only innate aptitude that can lead to more than average proficiency. The technical side of things can, as always, be mastered quite easily, but if there is no special talent all further efforts at improvement will be thrown away.

The astrological aspects to be found in our horoscopes reveal any disposition we may have for the theoretical or practical sides of the occult sciences – including the science of pendulum dowsing. In our own horoscopes we should look at the Ninth House and see whether it is occupied by Uranus and Neptune, or by one of these planets in favourable aspect with the other. What is more, these planets, if in the Ninth House, should also be strong by Sign. No doubt the important role played in magic by both Uranus and Neptune is general knowledge. Nevertheless, though extremely desirable, it is not absolutely essential for the Radix to be as described. Periods occur bringing transitory effects which make it easier for an individual to be successful in experiments with pendulum dowsing. The same is true of mirror and crystal magic, which we intend to discuss later on, and also of astral projection.

The aspects and places of Neptune and Uranus in our horoscope are of the greatest importance. Those whose horoscopes have both these planets favourably placed can achieve excellent results given enthusiasm and perseverance. Perhaps we should stress once more that it is not sufficient to be able to make the pendulum work; for worthwhile results one must possess certain qualities.

There are four kinds of radiation exerting a joint influence in pendulum dowsing. They come from the object over which the pendulum is held, from the material of which the pendulum bob is made, from surrounding articles and from the person who holds the pendulum in his or her hand.

In order to avoid faults and blunders, these four kinds of radiation must always be taken into account, with the realization that the results obtained can be affected by them. For reliable results one must proceed very circumspectly, and must appreciate that while, ultimately, all results are in keeping with one another, the manner in which they are obtained is variable. The many deviations in pendulum paths and diagrams which are encountered, even in the work of the most careful researchers, are explicable only by the interactions of the four main sources of radiation.

First of all, then, you must determine your own individual pendulum swing and you should always use this as your starting point. Several matters require attention in addition to talent and training. For accurate results, the strictest objectivity and composure, absolute honesty of purpose, stamina and self-control are necessary.

Every experiment has to be repeated on different occasions and the possibilities must be thoroughly explored. You should alter the circumstances in which the experiment takes place and on occasion should try the effect of introducing adverse factors. Do your dowsing at different times of day, under different astrological aspects and different atmospheres and, above all, avoid being influenced by your feelings to an excessive extent. When experimenting with the pendulum, the feelings and the understanding must be kept in balance, otherwise you may fall victim to your own eagerness and imagination. Another danger is one-sidedness. You could realize quite early on that your best results come to you from a certain direction; nevertheless, you should make sure that you do not lose sight of other possibilities. That this is no empty warning you may see for yourself by dipping into the available literature of the subject. You will come across many illogical conclusions and tortuous arguments. The reason for this is, in many cases, that the writers are consumed by ambition and are trying to go one better than one another when describing their personal results.

When dowsing over a photograph it is easy to forget that one has to do not only with the picture of a certain person but also with a photographic print, with a paper manufacturer, with a retailer and with the materials of which the photograph is made. All these factors have played a part in the making of the photograph and their vibrations are attached to it. Experienced dowsers have learnt by their mistakes and talk of infection by other photographs and/or articles.

So one must be cautious and objective when using the pendulum. By and by we shall see how photographs may be dowsed in a reliable manner, account being taken of all disturbing influences. You should also avoid the unnecessary investigation of things such as foodstuffs. One should not become too involved in the banalities of everyday life. The powers of the pendulum and your own time are too precious for this. The main interest is to dowse cosmic and human potentials; ¯all the rest may well be interesting to the researcher but is hardly of prime importance.

After all these preparatory considerations which, although they may have seemed long-winded, are absolutely necessary, you can begin your experiments. Presumably, you will have chosen an astrologically favourable moment; however, it will be just as satisfactory if you have taken the pendulum in your hand at a time you intuitively feel is 'right'. Find a quiet place where no one will disturb you and take off all metal objects such as rings, cuff-links, penknives, watches, etc. Many people find these precautions super-fluous, but it is better to take them initially. Later on, it is not so important to do so because you can be guided by experience.

Sit down at a wooden table which has been protected from the influence of the earth's magnetic radiations by standing its legs on glass saucers or in glass tumblers. All articles required for the experiment should be placed within arm's length on another table. The surface in front of you must be insulated with glass, rubber or linoleum; preferably with a pane of blue glass lying on a large rubber sheet.* By taking these precautions you will exclude possible sources of interference.

Sit facing the south when dowsing.

Coming now to the pendulum itself, we find that it can be made of any material, as for instance of gold, silver, iron, copper, bronze, glass, etc. Nevertheless, in the beginning, it is advisable to employ a pendulum made of some material ruled by your astrological sign. Copper is also particularly suitable because it is so sensitive to radiations.

As to shape, it is best to start with a bob that tapers to a pointed tip. See Figure 2 (c, d, e). In your initial experiments use a bob that is not too heavy, weighing between ⅓ and ½oz., say. It should be suspended on a silken thread or a hair so as to be 4 to 6 inches from

---

*It should perhaps be noted here that since rubber insulates dowsing radiations, many experts advise against the wearing of rubber-soled footwear during dowsing. In other words, the articles being dowsed should be insulated if possible but the dowser should not. This seems to be the general rule. However, those who due to some physical defect are suffering from an unnatural leakage of body magnetism may find the reverse is true.

Tr.

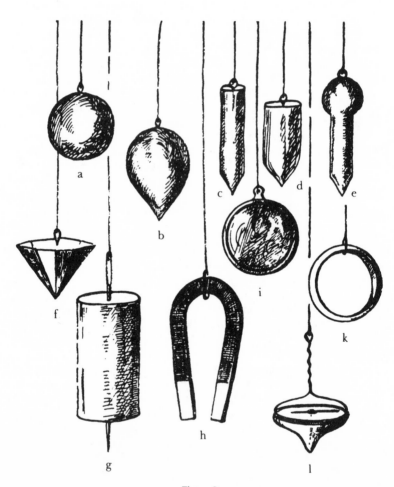

Figure 2.
(a) spherical pendulum (b) droplet pendulum (c) cylindrical pendulum
(d–e) conical pendulum (f) prism-shaped pendulum (g) cylinder and
needle (h) horseshoe magnet (i) coin (k) ring (l) compass.

the fingers. The thread must be at least as long as your forearm (from elbow to fist). When tying the thread, make certain that its end is not split, as this will in itself produce radiation.

The following method of holding the pendulum is recommended to beginners. Extend the forefinger and fold the thumb over the other fingers as they lie shut against the palm. Loop the pendulum thread round the first phalange of the forefinger, level with the nail, making sure it does not restrict the circulation of the blood. Resting your elbows firmly on the table, hold the pendulum a half to one inch above the article you are examining. Your body must be kept passive and relaxed. Every unnecessary tension of the muscles, especially those of the arm and hand, must be avoided.

Now a word about your mental attitude, which is even more important than your bodily one. Cultivate a feeling of anticipation without forming any particular expectations. Look for some response but do not try to think what it will be. At this stage it is so easy to let the emotions become involved and to tense up, but that is fatal to success. Mind and body must be fully relaxed and any superfluous inflow of energy must be prevented.

Pendulum dowsing is done with the right hand, even if the dowser is left-handed. The left hand is relaxed and held back with the thumb and fingers spread. These must not touch one another, otherwise their polarities may cause disturbances.

Now that all the precautions necessary for a favourable result have been taken, lay a piece of gold in front of you and wait quietly to see what will happen. The first movement of the pendulum will be something of a revelation to you. You will clearly sense that this movement is not being caused by you or by your arm or finger, but by an interplay of forces. These forces are very subtle and refined and it is their mutual relationship which induces the motion. You will become conscious of the mighty force-field of the cosmos; a force-field of which you are a part and which contains everything from the smallest to the greatest. Realize that you are now in a position actually to feel the force-field. After having inwardly experienced and assimilated the first pendulum experiment in accordance with the rules given above, you may proceed to systematic research. As you gain experience and fresh insights, you will be less subject to strict regulations. In professional dowsing the position of the hand and fingers will often be consciously adjusted to make the 'feeling' stronger.

For the purpose of making an exact study of the pendulum and so as to be able to recognize any divergences from its regular motion, you will have to make a pendulum disc as illustrated in Figure 3. By using your disc you can see whether or not the pattern described by

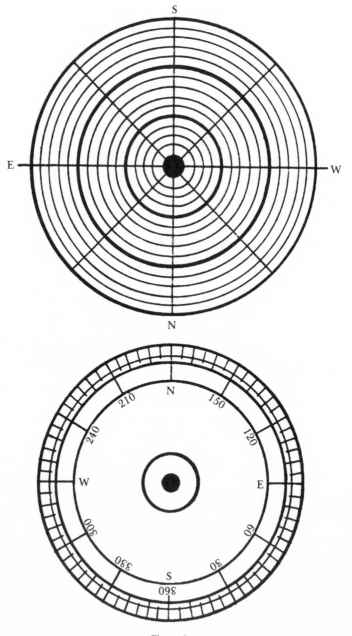

Figure 3.

the pendulum is being distorted in some way. Make a practice, right from the start, of noting all the data gleaned every time you dowse a given object so that you can compare your own results with those of others and thus assist your own development.

The pendulum can describe three sorts of figures: circles, ellipses and straight lines. The variability of these figures is very great however, as you will see from the examples in Figure 4.

Something else we should mention is this. When dowsing, direct your glance at the point of the pendulum, but do not describe an imaginary pendulum path with your eyes, for that could influence the results. All articles and equipment which you need for dowsing must be completely freed from foreign radiations to prevent the latter affecting what goes on.

To do this you can lay the article concerned in running water for some time, but another method is to magnetize it with your left hand. Hold this hand just above the object and draw a deep breath seven times. Each time you breath in, imagine that all foreign influences which may have attached themselves to the article to be cleansed are being absorbed by your magnetically polarized left hand during *inspiration*. Following these seven breaths shake your hand as if you were throwing off drops of water from it – in this way you will rid yourself of the Od taken up. Next hold the pendulum over the object and concentrate on the foreign influence. If the pendulum hangs still you will know that the influence is no longer there. Repeat the process with the insulated surface on which the object is to be placed. Only when all this has been done can you start to dowse. Due to this very undesirability of contamination by foreign influences, you should be careful not to let others handle your pendulum. Wear it on your person as much as possible and keep it wrapped in a black silk cloth. Charge the pendulum with Od before starting to dowse. This is done by holding it in your closed right hand and breathing on it three times. Behave with sufficient animation to saturate the pendulum with your own life-force. Never forget that your imagination is the most powerful tool you possess and that all magic is simply the result of the properly applied power of imagination.

Should you ever have to operate with a strange pendulum (avoid doing so as far as possible), do your best to remove the foreign Od as described above and to load the instrument with your own Od.

Our first series of experiments is concerned with the dowsing of minerals, and it involves finding not only the type of pattern traced out by the pendulum but the orientation of this pattern. That is to say, we can see firstly what figure the moving pendulum describes above a given object and secondly to which degree between 0° and

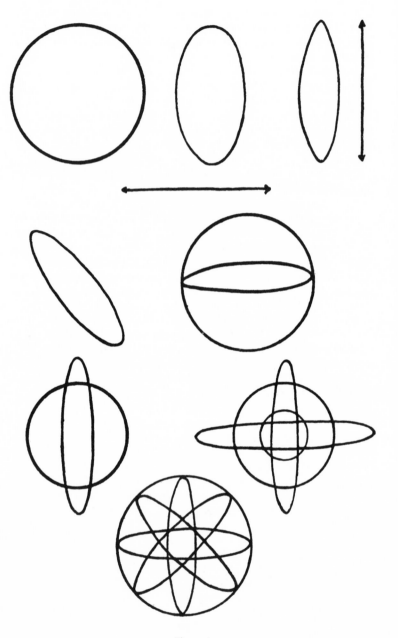

Figure 4.

360° the figure (ellipse or line) is turned. I shall give just a few examples here, to which you can add at will. However, do not spend too much time on this, because real pendulum magic is devoted to the detection of mental or spiritual radiations, and that is another story altogether.

Every development costs time, and proficiency with the pendulum is no exception. Therefore you must not skip these elementary exercises. Above all, do not lose your way in a mass of experimental possibilities, however interesting and important each may be in itself. Do not forget that your route is designed to take you to ether. The paths traced by the pendulum demonstrate our theory of transcendental images in the ether, which serve as moulds for groups of electrons.

Paint a number of sheets with water colours or take some coloured paper and see what figures the pendulum describes over the principal colours. On another page you will find two diagrams with which you may compare your results. But do look on these experiments as a transition phase. Now try dowsing a material with a pendulum made of the same material, i.e. gold with gold, silver with silver, copper with copper, and so on. You will be surprized by the results.

Record the results of all your pendulum work on sheets, with a careful note of the date, time, place, atmospheric conditions, etc.

Following these experiments you can proceed to dowse one substance using a pendulum made of another of a different sort. For example you can dowse with pendulums made of gold, copper, silver, iron, wood, ivory and so on over salt, earth, water, etc. Do not forget to take the necessary notes of course. When your own results have been compared with those of others and have been found to be in agreement with them, you may consider that you have really mastered the pendulum. At this point you will have fulfilled all the requirements which had to be met before you could move from the material sphere to the spiritual sphere. You no longer need to rest your arm on the table but are free in your movements. Your results will be easier to obtain and will be more accurate into the bargain.

The time has now come to pass from pattern dowsing to degree dowsing. For this purpose you will have to make a cardboard disc as illustrated in Figure 3, divided into degrees and marked with the four cardinal points of the compass. Every object has its own degree peculiar to itself, detectable by the pendulum given the proper mental adjustment of the pendulist. The tables printed here give examples of some of the most important substances and materials to enable you to check your orientation. However, they are no more than guidelines. If you have a special interest in this field of research

| Pendulum Material | Held over: | | | | | Metal |
	Iron	Nickel	Zinc	Copper	Lead	Alloy
Copper	↗	◯	↗	◯	◷	◯
Magnesium	↗	↗	↕	⬭	◑	↕
Rubber	↗	↕	⬭	↔	◯	◯
Gall-nut	↕	↗	↗	↔	◯	◯
Glass	◯	↗	↗	◯	◯	◯
Steel	↕	↗	⬭	↔	◯	◯
Silver	↗	↗	↗	↔	◯	◯

| Colour | Pendulum made of: | | | | | | |
	Copper	Magnesium	Rubber	Gall-nut	Glass	Steel	Silver
Lt. Blue	↔	⬭	◯	↕	↗	↔	◯
Dk. Blue	⬭	◑	↔	◯	↕	◷	↗
Green	◑	◯	↘	↙	◯	◷	◯
Red	◑	↗	◔	◯	◑	◯	◯
Black	◑	⬭	↔	↕	↔	◯	◑
Carmine	↗	◯	↕	◑	◯	◷	↔

because it affords surprising insights into numerology and can enlighten you on the way in which everything in the cosmos hangs together, you should try and consult *Der Dynamische Kreis* (The Dynamic Circle) by Johann Karl Bähr, published by Woldemar Türck at Dresden in 1861. Unfortunately, it is a book that is obtainable only through the second-hand trade.

3. Experiments and Exercises in Pendulum Magic

Pendulum magic, then, proves that real magic implies a control of cosmic forces. It is a responsible but typically human way of penetrating to the ultimate secret of the Logos, the number 1 or 'Being'. By carrying out these experiments step by step, you will find that your field of consciousness is incredibly expanded and you will discover how best to develop. By all means make yourself familiar with the literature of pendulum dowsing; in so doing you will save yourself a great deal of time and trouble. Now whether you extend your researches to the freely suspended pendulum or confine yourself to the fixed mounting pendulum described by Bähr and others – even if you go on to develop your own apparatus in order to protect the pendulum as much as possible from sources of disturbance in the human body (as Dr Maack did with his Manuradioscope) – is for you to decide. You may perhaps wish to specialize in some branch of the subject. Nevertheless, I do want to stress that, for our purposes, all this research into the nature of divining with the pendulum is important only by reason of its connection with magic. It is for this reason and this alone that you are striving to develop your skills.

As soon as you have mastered the art of dowsing for material objects, you should pass on to psychic dowsing. With this you leave the material world behind you and enter an entirely new realm where higher principles hold sway. The pendulum becomes a means of activating, conveying and setting free your own magical powers. The moment has at last come to talk about real pendulum magic.

You must understand, of course, that this too is a specialized subject. Even for the superficial dowsing of a piece of wood, some aptitude is needed if useful results are to be obtained. Everyone has a certain amount of this aptitude, but it is more developed in some of us than in others. It ought to be obvious that still greater ability is required for experiments involving a completely different, mental

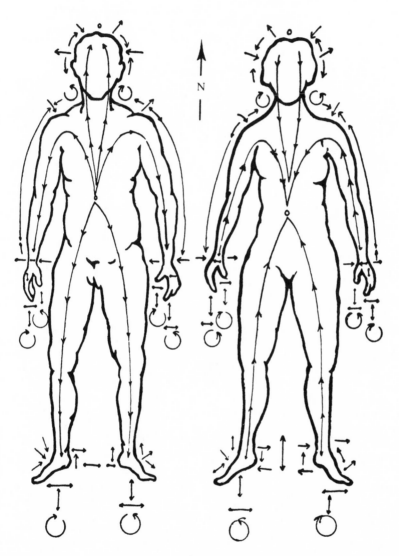

Figure 5.

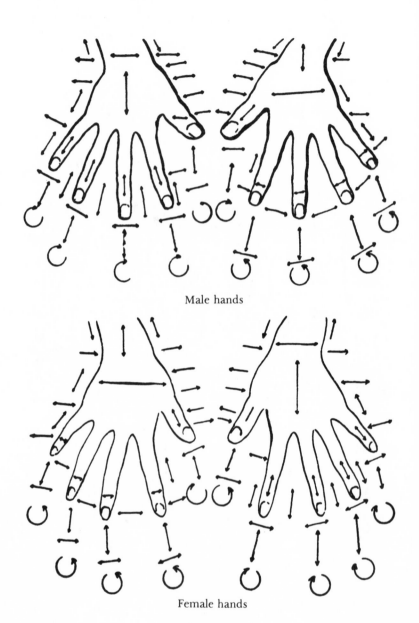

Male hands

Female hands

Figure 6.

or spiritual, set of phenomena. Be tireless, therefore, in the development of your dowsing talent. You know about human polarities; the pendulum can make them invisible to you after a fashion. Let us make a start then by taking a closer look at the dowsing of human beings.

Figures 5 and 6 give a clear picture of the specific pendulum patterns of man and woman.

The pendulum may be employed to investigate various parts of the body and the radiation strength will supply you with information about the sex, character and physical and emotional constitution of a person. The pendulum reacts most vigorously over the sex organs. In this way you can determine whether the polarity is wrong and whether there is a conflict between the sex and the psyche.

For example, when you find more ellipses than circles in a man, you may be sure that he tends to be effeminate and *vice versa*. This powerful action of the genitals is also important in the dowsing of astral entities and immediately shows whether you are dealing with a sun-force or a moon-force.

It is possible for the polarity to be completely reversed in an individual and, when this is the case, he must be treated quite differently from usual when being magnetized. This is a point to be watched when magical experiments are being carried out; otherwise the results will not be satisfactory. In sex magic in particular the polarity must be known. If a mistake is made, the medium will not be opened emotionally and any measures taken on the grounds of sexuality will miss the mark.

To find the true polarity, hold the pendulum over the individual's thumb. Normally, the pendulum will gyrate in wide circles. Over the left thumb the gyration must be clockwise and over the right thumb it must be anticlockwise.* A medium presenting a different picture from this is unfit for magical experiments.

Anyone who remembers the above advice will be saved from many disappointments. The pendulum is an excellent tool, with a big part to play in the success of magical practices. In addition it is especially suitable as an aid to obtaining reliable information about personality and character.

If you hold the pendulum with the right amount of mental concentration above the root of someone's nose you can discover the most prominent characteristics of his or her personality. Concentrate on the head and nerves. Normally, the pendulum will describe clockwise circles just as over the heart. The type of the circles will supply you with several clues. The number of circles, their size and sort are all important factors.

*Figure 6 seems to indicate that the reverse is true in women's hands.   *Tr.*

Now suspend the pendulum over the chest of your subject – you will detect the force being radiated by the lungs. Diseased patches show up where the pendulum comes to a complete standstill. When the pendulum seems to be pulled in the direction of a point that is usually top right, severe inflammation or some other trouble is indicated. A stoppage of the pendulum for at least ten minutes points to tissue destruction in the organ concerned.

THE REACTIONS OF THE PENDULUM OVER THE BODY

Cerebrum, face	O (Δ)	Intestines	O
Cerebellum, lower jaw, neck	O	Abdominal organs	←→
Apex of right lung	↘	Right leg, thigh	↕
Bronchial tubes	↕	Right leg, knee	O
Apex of left lung	↗	Right leg, shank	↓
Heart	O (Δ)	Left leg, thigh	↓
Lungs	O	Left leg, knee	O
Stomach	O	Left leg, shank	↓
Liver	O	Feet	O
Solar plexus	O	Vitality large or small circles	

Investigate the heart in the same manner. Normally you will get a quiet, even circular movement of the pendulum in a clockwise direction. Every deviation in the form of non-uniform movements or of a trembling or pulling sensation in the pendulum indicates irritability or disease of the heart. If the pendulum remains still for ten minutes or more the person is dead. However, form an opinion *very carefully* on this point, especially when dowsing photographs. The pendulum cannot lie or make mistakes, but you must use it with complete objectivity and must be absolutely certain that you are proficient in its employment.

Next examine the gastric region and the solar plexus. The large, wide circles made by the pendulum in this region demonstrate the importance of this nerve centre and give an insight into the functions and activity of the nervous system. Hold the pendulum over the body and you will get longways, wide ellipses. A little lower down, over the abdomen, the pendulum will swing in a clockwise, transverse ellipse in response to the purely vegetative life. Transverse ellipses are the norm here, though anywhere else in the body they are unfavourable. If the long axis of the ellipse does not cross the long axis of the body at right angles but lies across it obliquely, perverse tendencies are indicated according to Glahn. I myself have often found this to be true. Always be on the watch for such pointers. The arms and legs induce movements which are parallel to the limbs.

In the above manner you can dowse a person's photograph, handwriting and even his shadow. You will always obtain the same results.

The above experiments may be alternated with other tests on the radiation power of the body. There is no need to touch the place being studied; it is quite sufficient to point towards it with the bunched fingertips of the left hand. Remember that your mental attitude is very important here. You should achieve the same results as before, and you should also get the same results if you simply picture the organ or other part of the body to be studied in your mind and project as it were this mental image onto a blank sheet of paper that has previously been cleared of Od.

As soon as you have mastered the above exercises you can go on to dowse the most subtle radiations, irrespective of whether they are physical, emotional or mental. Thus you can come to know people's characters. Unfortunately, there is no space here to delve any deeper into this fascinating subject, so I must refer you to the literature of the subject and especially to the books of Frank Glahn. I have been able to confirm every single one of his results.

Of course there are other methods of reading character. To name but a few, we have astrology, phrenology, physiognomy and graphology. Character study by means of the pendulum is more in the nature of confirmation, but assumes importance in the absence of both an individual and his handwriting. In such circumstances you can form a mental image of him or her and project it on the sheet of paper in front of you.

The pendulum is also particularly suitable for determining the fundamental vibrations of thought forms, elementals or astral entities – regardless of whether or not these are 'good' or 'evil'. I intend to return to this subject and deal with it rather more fully, but that should not stop you from experimenting and drawing your own conclusions. Coming back to the question of character reading for a moment, I should perhaps say that differences of opinion exist as to the exact meaning of the reactions of the pendulum. There need be no surprise at this if you will consider how many different vibrations and graduations of vibrations go to make up the human personality.

Hold the pendulum over the centre of your subject's chest and concentrate on divining his character. First of all you will obtain the well-known circles and ellipses. If these are small and narrow, the character will be petty and narrow-minded. Movement along a perpendicular line indicates egotism, heartlessness and wilfulness. If the line is a long one and the pendulum swings upwards towards the head with considerable force, the person is energetic but unfeeling and ruthless. If the pendulum executes placid, wide circles and ellipses, there is much mental and constructive force present. Sometimes the figures described by the pendulum are small at first but gradually become wider. The meaning of this is that the person concerned has evolved spiritually to a higher level from his original petty-mindedness. The opposite is true when wide circles become smaller. A parallel can be found in the margins of letters in graphology, which have a similar significance according to whether they increase or decrease in width. Once again, you will observe how the pendulum confirms the results of other sciences. How could it be otherwise when although the ways are different they lead in the same direction?

Broad ellipses indicate a love of humanity. When the lines dip towards the feet, there is a great love of material things. If the circle described by the pendulum is somewhat depressed at the top, so that the cerebrum is left out of it, stupidity or a lack of mental energy is indicated. Where no spiritual personality is present, the individual concerned is conscious on the material level but has no realization of spiritual things. In that event, the pendulum describes just one type of figure: ellipses in women and circles in men – pointing to mere vegetative functions.

But all this has to be put into practice. Your findings will relate not only to vibrations emanating from coarse matter but also to vibrations emanating from fine matter. Even an astral plane entity can be detected in this way.

One thing that must always be borne in mind during all these experiments is that your own thought-waves and those of others can have a disturbing effect. You will appreciate that the pendulum is very sensitive to thought-waves. Because telepathic influence on the pendulum is one of the possibilities, you will have to take every precaution to exclude anything of the sort coming from yourself.

This is the place to mention yet another matter. All the atmospheres, emotions and vibrations of people and astral beings will be transferred to you and you will clearly feel their influence in the arm holding the pendulum. You know that when you use the pendulum Od-force is lost; besides this, however, there is an exchange of Od and an uptake of Od. Diseases, too, can be conveyed via the pendulum; so do not forget to protect yourself in the proper manner (with a 'cloak' of Od, a pentagram, magnetic breathing, etc.). When you are dealing with noble-minded, good individuals, the pendulum will gyrate in wide, uniform circles and the thread will not often be long enough to display these circles to their fullest extent. On the other hand, with malign individuals who are driven by their animal passions you will feel a certain amount of aversion and horror, your arm will go into a cramp, you will feel listless, the pendulum will fall from your hand and, sometimes, you will be unable to proceed.

Should you be affected in the above way, it is important for you to remove the infecting Od immediately and to commence rhythmic respiration in order to rid yourself of the negative vibrations which have taken possession of you. If, while using the pendulum on humans or other beings you feel a marked downward pull on it, you must regard this as unfavourable. The signs are even worse if this happens along the notorious east-west line. Also, incidental anti-clockwise gyration when character is being examined signals the presence of adverse tendencies.

You have now heard enough about this very specialized field of pendulum dowsing to set up your own experiments. In character dowsing you must reach your own conclusions on which you feel you may safely rely. Try to analyse your own character by intro-spection, record your various traits and see what patterns the pendulum gives for them. The results will be peculiar to yourself and will be correct. By proceeding as described you can achieve excellent results.

It should be clear to you that, with the help of your pendulum, you will be able to detect sympathy and antipathy – attraction and repulsion – between people, animals, plants and minerals. An enclosing circle always indicates sympathy, rapprochement and alliance. A separating line shows repulsion and antipathy.

If you wish to know whether two people will get on well with one another, suspend the pendulum between their two right hands. The result will answer your query. Similarly you can discover which materials you can safely use and which you can not. Place your hand on the table and put a small piece of tobacco beside it. Hold the pendulum over the space between them and concentrate mentally on attraction or repulsion.

Positive results with the substance concerned are given when the pendulum describes large circles which sometimes enclose the whole hand. In the other case, a line of demarcation is drawn between the hand and the object and makes it plain enough that you ought not to use the substance in question. In the same way you can test medicines for their kind and use and even discover whether they aid assimilation or secretion. If the movement of the pendulum starts from the remedy and the bob seems to be impelled towards the person concerned, the medicine will withdraw substances from the body and therefore promotes excretion. The same will be true of fruits and vegetables, and so you can check in advance what effect they are likely to have on you.

But if the pendulum is impelled away from the person and towards the remedy, the latter will have a fortifying action and will add substances to the body. You can check this on such things as milk, eggs, rice, potatoes, nuts and bread.

Divination of Disease

The divination of disease is a subject on its own. Proficiency in it demands deep study and all I can offer here are a few brief notes. I shall do no more than tell you a few things which have to be known by the practitioner of magic. The pendulum can inform you whether someone is hysterical, has poor nerves or is weak-minded. These points are very important to watch out for and avoid when one is looking for a medium.

Hysteria gives a nervy, lively path of the pendulum, which is rather 'excitable'. Weak nerves are indicated by lines running east and west which gradually grow shorter until the pendulum comes to a stop. A weak intellect is shown by nervy lines traced above the forehead, and when the pendulum comes to the end of its swing it behaves as it it had hit a solid wall from which it rebounds.

If the pendulum makes lively circles over the female breast then the woman is sexually active and the type of circles described shows in what direction her sexuality is aroused. This whole field of research waits to be explored and would afford you an opportunity to improve your skill.

The more you can tune in to each vibration the better your results will be and the easier it will become for you to detect and analyse the very finest vibrations.

The dowsing of colours and symbols is a further stage on the way to true pendulum magic. You must tune into the vibration of the colour you are studying and not into its composition. Dowsers differ in their findings here because their preconceived opinions, the conditions in which they are working and the sort of pendulum they are using can all affect the path traced out by the latter. The best plan is to classify your results and use these as a guide.

Another important practice is the divination of symbols. Symbols are cosmic powers bound to certain forms. There are many avenues of approach to the confirmation of your intuitive sense of their meaning by means of pendulum divination.

You could begin by discovering whether a given symbol contains good or evil forces, whether these forces are astral or mental and whether their vibrations are sympathetic or antipathetic to you or not. In addition, you could ascertain whether or not the symbol is a cosmic glyph or a human force. Hold the pendulum over such symbols as the triangle, circle, square, pentagram and hexagram (Solomon's Seal) and dowse the shape, colour and radiation of each. You will delve deeper into their essential natures and become more aware of the cosmic powers they symbolize.

The same method may be employed to dowse astrological symbols, characters, magical words or sigils, and even sounds, and thus to go on extending your understanding of cosmic laws.

In magical societies the astrological aspects and the strains they produce in the force-field of the human personality are sometimes studied with the aid of the pendulum. The true ascendant of the native of the horoscope is found in this way; also, the colours and sounds associated with given Zodiac signs and planets. These are things you yourself can do. They are quite striking experiments which will open your inner eye to the secrets of the cosmos.

The subject assumes considerable importance in magical training. All talismans and amulets* are bundles of extremely fine vibrations. The pendulum can inform you about the type of force being studied – that is to say, whether it attracts or repels, whether it has to do with white or black magic, whether it is protective or destructive – and can disclose to you the type and properties of the associated powers. It is very important to be able to say with certainty whether a talisman or amulet that you have not made yourself has or has not been made from the correct material and under the proper astrological influence. You will then be able to avoid mistakes and disappointments.

Dowsing Precious Stones

And now we come to the important question of dowsing precious stones. As you know, gems hold within themselves magical powers which are capable of influencing us either positively or negatively. Many well-accredited historical facts could be quoted in support of this. It is therefore important to know the appropriate stone for a given magical activity.

*Talismans attract positive forces, whereas amulets ward off negative ones (Note in Dutch edition).

In these days when synthetic stones are being made which even the expert finds difficult to distinguish from the genuine article, so alike are they in composition, weight, hardness and other properties, the pendulum is a great asset.

The instrument's reactions leave nothing to be desired. When you concentrate on the life-force of the stone, you will get a clear response if the stone is genuine, but over a false stone the pendulum hangs motionless. All the pendulum can do for imitation gems is to say of what chemical substances they are composed. At the end of this section on pendulum magic you will find a table giving the degree through which the pendulum swings when held over the main precious stones, elements, colours and other items. It should prove useful to you in your own experiments.

In all experiments with the pendulum so far described, you should adhere to the working method laid down in the first exercise. It will provide you with a secure basis for developing your skill and your mental adjustment. Eventually you can alter your finger-hold in order to discover the most sensitive way for you of suspending the pendulum, so that you can pick up the finest vibrations. Figure 7 illustrates several possibilities. For coarse vibrations, the first two finger-holds in Figure 7 are best, and a conical or cylindrical pendulum should be used; the pendulum bob needs to have a large surface area and considerable weight in order to 'pick up' the force-fields properly and then to react to them. The finer and more subtle the vibrations, the smaller must be the pendulum and the more delicately balanced must be the finger-hold in order to tune it in to the cosmic radiations.

As you penetrate into the mysterious and largely uncharted realms of the pendulum, you will discover more new methods for making tests and will equip yourself more thoroughly for working pendulum magic.

To dowse the radiations of Od coming from the human aura, proceed as follows. Lay the naked test subject along the magnetic meridian with his head to the north and his feet to the south, taking the usual precautions (i.e. place blocks of glass under the legs of the bed and cover the mattress with a rubber sheet).* Make yourself completely passive both physically and mentally and commence dowsing.

You can now do one of two things: either you can pass your left

*This is only a suggestion, for what it is worth, but it is possible that the above arrangement (duplicating what was said earlier in the book about protecting the area in which inanimate objects are dowsed), might serve to shield sleepers from harmful earth-radiations where these have been found by dowsing.   Tr.

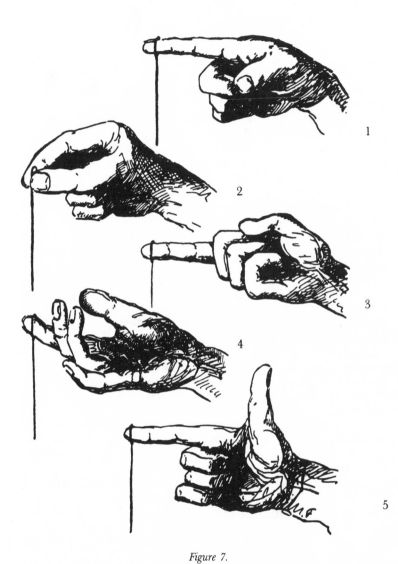

Figure 7.

hand four to twelve inches above the subject's body while concentrating on the radiations of Od, or else you can suspend the pendulum bob itself at the same height above his body. Note the figures traced out by the pendulum over individuals in sickness and in health. Your results will be peculiar to yourself and it is for you to discover your own reactions. Concentrate on the nodal points of the life-force, such as the solar plexus, the pineal gland, the heart and the sex organs.

Do the same thing with sleeping subjects and with those who are just waking, with magnetized individuals and with mediums who have entered a trance. Record your findings carefully; they are highly important and will assist you in your magical experiments.

Once you are familiar with the simple potential differences between the radiations of Od from the human body, it will be easy for you to distinguish between radiations of Od and other, external radiations – a very important matter. Carefully study the potential around the sex organs; in this way you can determine the nature and strength of an individual's sex drive. Both mental and physical impotence reveal themselves to the pendulist and sometimes his is the only method that will reveal the cause of this type of trouble, beset as it is with so many mysteries. In all your experiments, the test-subject must be undressed, as already stated.

The life-force in the human sperm may also be examined. Even in sexual magic the pendulum can bring improved results. The impact of menstruation on a woman's force-field is also clearly revealed by the pendulum. Evidently, menstruation not only eliminates waste matter from the body but produces a parallel cleansing of the sexual aura while, at the same time, leading to the accumulation and storage of fresh Od-force in the womb in readiness to environ a new life. Here the pendulum puts us in touch with the profoundest mysteries of procreation, embryology and maternity.

The pendulum will unfailingly show whether or not a person is a virgin, and that is another area for your experimentation. Nevertheless, as soon as you have gained confidence, you should go on to dowse for thoughts and thought-forms.

Begin by tuning your experiments in to the suggestion being made by a hypnotist to his subject. As soon as the vibrations sent out impinge on the pendulum, the latter starts to swing, revealing the thought-force being projected at his subject by the hypnotist. It is thus that an exchange of Od takes place between waking or sleeping individuals.

By means of these experiments you may be able to detect the force-fields photographed by Dr Baraduc and others. The pendulum will help you to determine their shape, nature and colour. The following method is recommended.

Let someone who has been trained in the practice, passively retain a certain thought or series of thoughts, say a prayer, a mantram or a meditation. Now use the pendulum to find the form and colour of the psychic field surrounding the subject's head. What you will pick up are the thought-waves emitted by a person during meditation.

Now start to create independent thought-forms in order to dowse their form and type of vibration. Here is an example of what we mean. Cleanse the room in which you are working of all foreign vibrations (by burning incense in it, by removing its Od etc.), and by using extreme concentration and kneading the Od-force with your hands, so to speak, make a thought-form of a certain shape, a ball say, and then try to detect it with the pendulum. Get a number of people who know what to do to create a number of similar forms, and without knowing where they are try to locate these in the room by means of the pendulum and to work out their nature and shape. In this case, make use of the finger-holds pictured in Figure 7 (3, 4, 5) and use your open left hand as an antenna.

By direct awareness of warmth or coldness your hand will inform you where the thought-forms in question are positioned; the pendulum will then go on to reveal their type and quality. Always write up your results, as they will prove useful in helping you to distinguish the vibrations you will encounter in your subsequent investigations. So you see, you can search an appartment for the thought-forms created by others, whether these individuals are absent or present, and can achieve a greater understanding of the experiences and feelings of sensitive people.

All is radiation, all is vibration, making up the whole of Being and governed by cosmic laws. Man is a unique force-field, equipped with a consciousness that can think and feel and that therefore is able to recognize the nature of all things. Slowly but surely you will develop, becoming more and more aware of the 'divine spark'. Your development is that of mankind itself. We are journeying together and our goal is eternity.

TABLE OF DYNAMIC VALUES

Elements:		Precious stones:	
hydrogen	0°	lapis lazuli	290°
gold	0°	sapphire	322.5°
diamond	5°	beryl	290°
silver	45°	emerald	297.5°
zinc	67.5°	aquamarine	300°
palladium	90°	emerald, light green	302.5°
uranium	100°	chrysoberyl	305°
copper	112.5°	jacinth, pale red	305°
iridium	120°	jacinth, dark red	315°
tin	125°	grey tourmaline	272.5°
aluminium	130°	black tourmaline	290°
platinum	135°	ruby	312°, 315°
nickel	140°		
cobalt	145°	Colours:	
lead	150°	cobalt blue	315°
iron	157.5°	indigo blue	255°
selenium	175°	aniline blue	217.5°
phosphorus	177.5°	aniline orange	222.5°
sulphur	180°	aniline red	215°
mercury	270°	aniline violet	230°
nitrogen	270°	aniline brown	240°
chlorine	355°		
oxygen	360°	Miscellaneous:	
		hydrogen	0°
Precious stones:		ice, snow	202.5°
diamond	5°	rainwater, distilled	
chrysolite	247.5°	water	180°
opal	247.5°	brass	ca. 105°
pure rock crystal	267.5°	half silver, half copper	77.5°
common quartz	270°	cast iron	150°
chalcedony	270°	English steel	152.5°
red tourmaline	280°	lodestone	330°
garnet	292.5°	humus	292.5°
jasper	295°	caffeine	265°
smoky topaz	297.5°	morphine	292.5°
fine tourmaline	290°		

PART TWO: CRYSTAL AND MIRROR MAGIC
4. Preparations

Dear Friend,

Perhaps you are rather surprised to receive a letter from me, but I have some time to spare at the moment and should like to devote it to you since you are my best and most diligent student. As you probably know, the Brotherhood has great things in store for you if you maintain your present rate of progress.

The prospect of instructing you further is a real pleasure since so far you have never disappointed me. Therefore I hope you will continue to abide by the rules and instructions of our Brotherhood so as to spend your days and nights in the eternal rhythm of the great laws. You are already vibrating in the cosmic circle in which there is no beginning and no end.

As I write this, I am sitting quietly in my cabin on board ship. The regular pounding of the engines does not disturb me. Gazing reflectively through the port-hole at the ocean, I am impressed by a wonderful dark red gleam that lies upon it such as is so seldom seen. It is that coppery red which can be observed during very special practices as a sign that a high degree of empathy has been achieved. You would not yet be able to endure the sight of this particular shade of colour without suffering from a sense of confusion. I am attuning my breathing and my pulse-rate to the motion of the waves, and the round pane of glass in my port-hole serves me as a magic mirror. One of the things I saw as I concentrated on it was you yourself at your evening exercises, but I saw something else invisible to you and that was the being standing next to you, attracted by your exercises and gaining in vitality as he fed on your Od-force. You had no idea of the danger threatening you but I know that spirit, who has been vibrating in one of the deepest astral worlds since the thirteenth century of our era. The Vâyu Tattva you had chosen for your exercises was not favourable for him, otherwise you would have beheld him.

As a matter of fact, this experience was what finally prompted me to write to you. I felt it was imperative to warn you that you must take more care to protect yourself. Certainly, your way leads you through these astral worlds but, as you already know, it is not in these your destination lies – it is much higher.

Therefore, I thought I would write something for you about the sort of magic that makes use of mirrors and crystal balls, of which you are still fairly ignorant.

Our Western literature has little enough to say about this kind of magic, and what it does say is largely incorrect. Even in the archives of the lodges of initiates there are books from which it is no longer possible to glean the truths deliberately hidden in them by the Masters, because the keys have been lost or forgotten. Accordingly, I hope you will take note of what I am going to tell you.

Do not forget how important are motives and goals. We are dealing here with the relationship between the forces anchored within you when they are consciously used, also with the definite repercussion of their radiations on yourself and on your astral body in particular. Your will should be absolute in this case. As soon as you have gained control over the place on which you have entered, you are its potentate within the limits of your comprehension of it. Of course, you will require prior training in order to withstand the opposing force in Âtma with your spiritual powers. But enough of this for now; your present task is to absorb what is stated here until the time comes for you to be given more precise instructions.

Natural magic mirrors exist in the form of the reflecting surfaces of still or slowly running water. They are very serviceable, especially at full moon but also during the waning moon, all according to the nature of the magical intention. The full moon is good for sympathetic or wish magic. The waning moon will take away diseases if you submerge your arms up to the elbows in running water. The waxing moon favours wish and thought transferences and releases them with sudden intensity when she is full.

So remember: full moon is the best phase for working quick and direct magic, but when the moon is waning the power available for magical transference decreases from day to day.

In any experiments you undertake pay strict attention to the breathing and concentration exercises I taught you. Results will come only with the hard training of your will. Find out which you need to practise the more: concentration or meditation. Always take into account that the person you want to contact or influence may be just as well trained as you are and may be protected by a mantle of Od, a talisman or some other piece of magic. Therefore you must not neglect to wear your own mantle of Od or to bind a pentagram on your forehead with a silken cord. Guard your solar plexus with the talisman I gave you and bear in mind that all forces emitted will return if they do not or can not reach their target or if their action is disturbed; in this event you will suffer harm if you are unprotected. The five-pointed star will ward off the invisible astral forces which are always present where magical experiments are in progress. Do not forget to fumigate the parchment on which, using intense concentration, you have inked the pentagram in black. The incense you employ must be previously charged with Odic force.

When you are attempting to project an influence, you must erect the pentagram as follows:

In magical invocations the pentagram is inverted, for then demonic forces are being attracted. But magicians take care to wear the upright five-pointed star over their solar plexi so that they themselves will not be injured.

Implements used for magic must not be used for any other purpose and must always be re-charged with Od-force before they are employed.

Here is an accurate moon table for reference:

The moon in the sign	Magically favourable when Ascendant is
♏ ♋ ♓	♍ ♏ ♉ ♋ ♓ ♌
♒ ♊ ♎	♈ ♊ ♌ ♎ ♐ ♒
♌ ♐ ♈	♊ ♌ ♎ ♐ ♒ ♈
♉ ♍ ♌	♋ ♍ ♏ ♌ ♓ ♉

To continue, it is essential to know what Tattva is active at the time of the experiment, for which purpose the following table should prove useful:

Tattva	Exercise	Experiment	Plane
Âpas	meditation	inner work	mental
Prithivi	meditation	inner work	mental
Tejas	concentration	influencing	astral
Vayu	concentration	conjuration	astral
Akâsha	concentration	conjuration	astral

You know that the positions of the moon and planets are of the utmost importance in all magical work and so should make a point of being accurate in your astrological calculations because certain entities do not vibrate unless the aspects suit them. Having studied astrology you should be able to perform the said calculations without error. Study your personal horoscope before going any further to see how the planets were placed at your birth. The following table will provide a few pointers:

Planet	Sign	Magically favourable aspects	In conjurations	For meditations
♄	♏ ♑ ♒	☌ ☽ ☍ ♅ ♀	□ ☽ ♅	
♀	♑ ♉ ♎ ♏	☌ ☽ ☍ ♅	☌ ♂ ♄	
☿	♑ ♐ ♒ ♏ ♋	☌ ☽ ♄	☌ ☿ ♄ □ ♄ ☽	△ ♃ ♂ ♀
☉	♑ ♐ ♒ ♏	☌ ☽ ♄ ♅ ♀	☌ ♄ ☽ ♅	△ ♀
☽	♏ ♒ ♓ ♋ ♊	☌ ♄ ♅ ♁	☌ ♄ ♅ □ ♄ ♀ ♅	△ ♃
♂	♏ ♑	☌ ♀	□ ♄ ♅	

Traditionally, magicians wear a hooded cloak made of silk over their naked bodies during all their exercises, meditations and experiments, since silk has an insulating function in magic, warding off foreign radiations and protecting their personal Odic force. The colours for this garment are as follows:

For conjurations	black silk
For magical influence	yellow silk
For sex magic	red silk
For religious ceremonies	purple silk

The hooded cloak is meant in general to cover every part of the body except the face.

The prescribed fast must be strictly observed before all ceremonies except those involving a release of considerable physical energy.

The failure of so many magical and ceremonial experiments is due to the fact that neophytes do not obey the instructions in every detail. Dilettantes have no notion of meticulous attention to detail: they usually trifle with low, sympathetic magic and their results are very hit-and-miss.

Magic mirrors are employed with various intentions. They can attract or repel certain forces, also they can serve as a means of concentrating and radiating such forces.

After use, the mirror must always be covered with a black silk cloth and must be stored in a dark place along with the other occult instruments (the latter need not be loaded with Odic force). It must be inaccessible to the uninitiated.

The mirror itself should be made of cut glass and coated on the back with mercury or black tar. It must be round and must not magnify. Coloured glass should not be used for it unless it is intended for healing purposes. Instead of cut glass, a highly polished steel disc can be employed. Even so, it must have the same coating as mentioned above on its back, because the said coating absorbs and retains the radiated Od.

Allow no one else to peer into your mirror, not even a fellow-student, and certainly not once the mirror has been prepared for magical experiments; because being charged with your personal Odic force it offers a ready gateway into your inmost personality.

The talent for achieving good results, especially in crystal magic, varies from person to person. The best Signs for magic, especially when the moon occupies them, are:

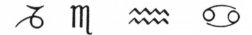

Spectacles or finery may not be worn during the experiments, nor may any jewels except for certain magical stones and talismans. The magician's black oak table and chair are previously charged with Odic force and then, with deep concentration, he chalks a white magic circle round him on the floor, closing it behind him. This he must on no account leave.

5. The Practice of Scrying

In conjurations with a higher purpose, the magician turns to face the west, in religious ceremonies he faces the east and in all other cases he sets his chair down on the north side so as to face south in line with the vibrations of the earth's magnetic aura. If he has to leave his magic circle unexpectedly, he always does so by way of the five-pointed star illustrated in the diagram (page 55), but he must never walk out backwards. One of the functions of a magic circle is to keep undesirable influences on the outside where they can not touch the operator; so, however efficiently he may imagine he has dismissed such influences from the vicinity before leaving the circle, he may when doing so enter their field of force. Therefore he must continue to wear the parchment seal on his forehead for a long time after the experiment is over and he has left the magic circle. *The strictest attention must be paid to this rule.* Remember: If you play with magic, magic will play with you. So, be warned.

The effect of what is being done is often enhanced if a good ethereal oil is rubbed into the forehead, the nape of the neck and the solar plexus before the ceremony is performed. The table has to be covered with a cloth of black silk or black velvet and the same is true of the chair or stool. For elementary experiments with mirror magic, the circle illustrated overleaf is quite adequate, but in genuine conjurations the arrangements are much more complicated.

If you are thinking of seeing spirits you must ask me for further instructions; which I shall give you provided I am satisfied with your account of what you are intending to do. High magic demands additional preparations, but pay no attention to the old grimoires as a great deal of dangerous nonsense was printed in them.

Burning the proper incense is important for the success of a given experiment. Pure ingredients and wood charcoal must always be used. Examples of the perfumes used are juniper twigs for Saturn,

Figure 8

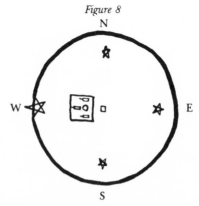

cummin for the Moon, saffron for Neptune, alder for Uranus, verbena for Venus, lavender for Jupiter, gorse for Mars, camphor for the Sun and thyme for Mercury. The perfumes for the Signs of the Zodiac are anise for Aries, aloes for Taurus, dill for Gemini, poppy seed for Cancer, clove for Leo, lime flowers for Virgo, jasmine for Libra, woodruff for Scorpio, sage for Sagittarius, rose-hip for Capricorn, lilac for Aquarius, willow for Pisces. The lists of fumigations in the possession of the Brotherhood are more detailed than· this but many of the ingredients mentioned are no longer considered to be suitable for use.

The perfumes of the Signs can be mixed with those of their ruling planets for the sake of completeness if so desired. The quantities used are from ⅓ to ¾ oz. in each case.

Experiments are preferably performed in front of an open window so that the moonlight can fall on the crystal ball or mirror. If this is not possible, consecrated wax candles are used and the table is laid as follows:

Figure 9.

The candles are arranged in a triangle and in such a way that their rays strike the ball or mirror to form a single point of light. On the left hand stands the censer. Care has to be taken that there are no reflections from any articles in the room in the ball or mirror. All prints and paintings must be removed from the walls. In advanced work the wand is held in the right hand, but this is a refinement and not essential for the little experiments we are contemplating now.

When all has been properly prepared and the scryer is sitting completely relaxed in his well-practised yoga asana, with controlled breathing, steady pulse rate and no spasmodic movements of the eyes or limbs, he will soon observe that the surface of the mirror or ball changes to a whitish or greyish disc that is faintly illuminated. The candle-light disappears from view and the disc starts to revolve slowly. This is the first stage. The scryer must take care not to fall asleep at this point because the turning disc has great hypnotic power and easily induces slumber. After a while, misty figures start to form in the milky white disc and he sees pictures of the people on whom he had been concentrating in the situations and places where they are at the moment of the experiment.

This is the second stage, when time and distance no longer matter. Sympathetic magic is now possible, of which more anon. The scryer can also try by the so-called splitting of the astral body to make the person concerned appear before him. I shall come back to this in a later letter, although your training in the arts of hypnosis and suggestion will have already given you a few clues as to the possibilities. When in this separated condition, the scryer must make sure that he cannot be disturbed by others or else, by the phenomenon of repercussion as it is called, the link between his physical and his subtle body will be disturbed or severed and he might die. Do not forget to study astrology as much as possible because it is the cornerstone of the whole magical edifice and the foundation of the Brotherhood's cosmic knowledge.

Your crystal ball must be fashioned from pure rock crystal or polished nickel. Admittedly, results can be achieved with hollow glass globes filled with distilled water, but to a lesser extent than with the genuine crystal ball. A crystal ball or stone that has been used by someone else should never be employed, nor should a crystal ball or stone given as a present. The Brotherhood possesses specially prepared magic mirrors made of two thinly sliced discs of rock crystal, between which there is enclosed a fluid of a particular composition. Scryers are advised to make their own magic mirrors.

Occasionally, the forms seen in the mirror or ball will appear to be standing on their heads. This is no cause for concern; it is merely due to a reversal of the optical reflexes.

Now for something which might not be anticipated by the amateur scryer, and that is the possibility that when he looks up he will see strange and grotesque apparitions surrounding him. These are no hallucinations, but elementals. They can do him no harm as long as his magic circle has been tightly drawn because they are not able to step across it. They are usually small and no attention should be paid to them, whether they are hovering in the air or creeping along the ground. Nor should any attention be paid to the hideous animal shapes which sometimes appear. However, if there appear in the mirror or crystal ball or even in the room itself, beings which are distinguishable from those we have just been considering, if not in their external appearance, then certainly in their vibrations, which register quite sharply in the scryer's nervous plexus at the same time as his nerves respond to the presence of an astral being with an immediate sensation of cold, then a previously prepared pentagram (placed at the scryer's right hand in readiness for this very contingency) must be held up to the entity while the scryer says in a resolute tone of voice, 'I command you to depart.' He does not have to say these words out loud (indeed the first time this sort of thing happens he will probably be unable to do so); it is enough for him to think them with mental concentration.

Tattva	Exercise	Experiment	Plane	Planet
Âpas	meditation	inner work	mental	Moon, Neptune, Venus
Prithivi	meditation	inner work	mental	Jupiter, Mercury
Tejas	concentration	influencing	astral	Mars, Sun, Venus
Vâyu	concentration	conjuration	astral	Uranus, Mercury, Moon
Âkâsha	concentration	conjuration	astral	Saturn, Neptune Moon

A clock ought to be on hand so that a calculation can be made of the Tattva ruling at the time when the entity made itself visible. It is important to make a note of the time.*

* Nothing is said here about how to calculate the ruling Tattva from the time of day. Occult writers seem to agree that the Tattvic flow starts at sunrise but usually fail to supply further details. Mrs E.A. Fletcher tells us in her book, *The Law of Rhythmic Breath* (Rider, 1908) that, 'According to the *Shivâgama*, the flow of the *Tattvas* is "Ghari by Ghari" (about twenty-four minutes), one after the other,' adding that, in this context, 'the flow of the *Tattvas* applies to their change in the solar and terrestrial currents of Prâna, and not at all to those in the human physique.' She then describes how the

I feel I should discontinue my explanations at this point and defer consideration of anything beyond the first two stages for the time being. I do not want you experimenting on your own initiative without being able to control the phenomena described above; and controlling them means being able to banish them at will. This you must do straight away; never fall into the trap of amusing yourself with apparitions which come to you unbidden. I cannot stress this rule too strongly.

With experience, the scryer learns the difference between the various types of imagery appearing in his crystal mirror or ball. Sometimes there are wish-fulfilment pictures or visions of the future, usually in symbolic form requiring interpretation. Then there are flash-backs to what appear to be past lives. Most of us get no further than so-called symbolic clairvoyance, which frequently leads to erroneous conclusions.

The wonderful properties of the magic mirror were proclaimed and studied by the ancient mystery schools. A harmonic relationship exists between colours and mirrors. By harmonious or inharmonious adjustment, a strong influence can be brought to bear on the human organism on the one hand and on the astral body on the other hand, the latter being more strongly bound in this way to the vibrations directed towards it by a trained will.

The following are the appropriate colour schemes used for chambers housing magic mirrors.

Planet	Colour	Sign	Colour
☉	Orange, golden brown	≈	grey
☽	White, silvery grey, violet, green	♓	blue-red, grey
☿	Light grey, pale yellow	♈	violet
♀	Pink, light green, light blue yellow	♉	blue
♃	Purple, dark blue	♋	light green
♄	Black, dark grey, dark brown dark green	♌	pale yellow
		♍	golden yellow
♅	Violet, lilac	♎	orange
♅	Grey, dark yellow	♏	red
♆	Green	♐	brownish red
		♑	greyish red

Tattvas flow in the human body, but that does not concern us here. The sunrise cycle starts with *Âkâsha* and then runs through *Vâyu, Tejas, Âpas* and *Prithivi*, when the cycle recommences.   *Tr.*

The colours of the Zodiac are those belonging to the dawning Aquarian Age. We never use colours which, at the moment of the experiment, do not harmonize with the rising signs and planets in the horoscopes of those concerned. As you see, so many things have to be taken into consideration during magical experiments.

The wall hangings are made of smooth, heavy silk that is not too glossy and it is advantageous to prepare a false ceiling of silk so as to conceal and dim the electric lighting. Wall-to-wall carpeting is another requirement. Some rooms have tall mirrors running from floor to ceiling in the middle of each wall so that their mutual reflections give the impression of endless roads passing through countless dark and mysterious caverns. Each chamber must be fumigated prior to use as indicated earlier. Such rooms easily induce or aid a state of trance because the action of the mirrors is so powerful and, indeed, can go on working in the subconscious for a long time. Never enter the room without wearing your magical garments as already described.

A black room is always employed on Saturday night, because that is Saturn's day. The same applies to all magical colour and mirror rooms. The perfume of the day is the only thing that changes. A red room is best for Fridays. For the rest, refer to the instructions already given.

Diseases can be alleviated in a yellow room, according to the astrological aspects.

A blue room is suitable only for religious exercises and meditations. Meditation and trance can be promoted by the beating of a gong at regular intervals precisely timed to the note at which the planet of the day vibrates. In religious ceremonies the arrangement of the mirrors can be altered so that three only are used to form the corners of an equilateral triangle.

Black or red rooms are used for summoning beings from the astral plane, but this is a procedure fraught with danger for the tyro.

Well, my friend, the time has come for me to close. I know that you will study my instructions carefully without being in too much of a hurry to put them into practice. Your intuition will usually tell you the best way to tackle things. Steel yourself to be unafraid in the face of strange forces from unknown spheres. Always remember that you yourself are the mirror image of a force vibrating on a higher plane and that therefore you should exercise mastery over the physical plane. When you realize this fact you will approach the deep occult knowledge that can govern the universal power known as Vril.

Go your appointed way in this incarnation wrapped in silence.